Three in the Back,
Two in the Head

a play by Jason Sherman

Playwrights Canada Press acknowledges the support of The Canada Council for the Arts for our publishing programme
and the Ontario Arts Council.

Cover: Ron White, Tarragon Theatre, Toronto, 1994
Photo: John M. Currid. Cover design - Tony Hamill

Canadian Cataloguing in Publication Data
Jason Sherman, 1962
        Three in the back, two in the head
A play
ISBN 0-88754-534-3
I. Title.
PS8587.H47T47 1995   C812'.54   C95-930772-9
PR9199.3.S44T47   1995

First edition: 1995. First printing 1996. Second printing, September 1999.
Printed and bound by Hignell Printing at Winnipeg, Manitoba, Canada.

Three in the Back,
Two in the Head

Playwrights Canada Press
Toronto • Canada

For Richard & Kugler

Jason Sherman's other plays include *The League of Nathans* (produced by Orange Dog Theatre in association with Theatre Passe Muraille, 1991), *Stop Slowing Down* (Rule Five Theatre/The Fringe of Toronto Festival, 1994), *A Place Like Pamela* (Walking Shadow Theatre, Toronto, 1990) and the collective *To Cry is Not So* (Theatre Smith-Gilmour, 1990). *The League of Nathans* received the 1992 Chalmers Award and was nominated for a Dora Mavor Moore Award for Outstanding New Play, as was *Three in the Back, Two in the Head.* Jason Sherman is the editor of two anthologies for Coach House Press, *Canadian Brash* (1990) and *Solo* (1994), a collection of one-person plays. From 1985 to 1990, he edited *what,* a literary magazine. He has been a playwright-in-residence with Necessary Angel Theatre Company and Theatre Smith-Gilmour and is playwright-in-residence at Tarragon Theatre.

Production History

Three in the Back, Two in the Head was commissioned by the Necessary Angel Theatre Company, through the Pilot Project program, and was developed over a three-year period, under the guidance of Richard Rose and D.D. Kugler.

In May 1993, *Three in the Back, Two in the Head* received a five-week workshop through Tarragon Theatre's Public Workshop program. The cast was: Michael Healey, Diana Leblanc, John Gilbert, Ken James and David Jansen. Richard Rose directed, D.D. Kugler dramaturged, Susan Monis stage managed and André Czernohorsky was the assistant director.

Three in the Back, Two in the Head was co-produced by Necessary Angel Theatre Company /Tarragon Theatre/National Arts Centre in January 1994 (at Tarragon Theatre in Toronto) and February, 1994 (at the National Arts Centre in Ottawa). The cast was:

PAUL JACKSON	*Michael Healey*
JOHN DOYLE	*Ron White*
ED SPARROW	*Guy Bannerman*
DONALD JACKSON	*Ken James*
ANNA JACKSON	*Carole Galloway*

Director - Richard Rose
Dramaturg - DD Kugler
Stage Manager - Susan Monis
Assistant Director - André Czernohorsky
Set and Lights - Graeme S. Thomson
Costumes - Charlotte Dean

Three in the Back, Two in the Head was substantially revised for the Carnegie-Mellon University Showcase of New Plays in Pittsburgh, PA., July, 1994. The cast was:

PAUL JACKSON	*Michael Waller*
JOHN DOYLE	*Randell Haynes*
ED SPARROW	*Larry John Meyers*
DONALD JACKSON	*Burt Edwards*
ANNA JACKSON	*Caitlin Hart*

Director - Brian Kulick
Stage Manager - Kelly Yann

Acknowledgements

The advice and support of Urjo Kareda, Artistic Director of Tarragon
Theatre, was, as always, concise, precise and invaluable. The comments
of all those who participated in the workshop and readings, as well as
those who attended them, have been most helpful. The play could not
have been written without the on-going support of several people. I
especially want to thank Jerry Doiron at Necessary Angel, Mallory
Gilbert at Tarragon, and Frank Gagliano and Mary Lou Chlipala at
Carnegie-Mellon. Special thanks are due Melinda Little, whose
generosity in all things is beyond compare. I would also be guilty of
taking for granted, were I not to mention them, the support of the
Canada Council, the Ontario Arts Council and the Toronto Arts
Council.

Note:

This play is a work of fiction. Though inspired by the death of an
actual person, it is solely the work of the playwright's imagination, and
does not in any way portray the character, actions, thoughts or words of
any persons, living or dead.

Scene One

Office of JOHN DOYLE, CIA Officer, Langley,
Virginia: DOYLE and PAUL JACKSON.

PAUL   I mean what did he do that—

DOYLE   What did he *do*, he—

PAUL   What was so wrong with what he did, with—

DOYLE   What he did was, as far as I can tell, just, from reading the papers, from, you know, the *Times* the, what, the *Post*, what he did was, he made guns, he sold guns and missiles and he, okay?, made missiles and—he "lived by the gun" and, callous though—

PAUL   No.

DOYLE   — callous though it may sound, he "died by the"—

PAUL   No, that's, "sold guns and miss—" I can't—

DOYLE   Do you—

PAUL   That's—

DOYLE   Do you deny—

PAUL   He was a scien—

DOYLE　　He lived in that world, he died in that world—

PAUL　　He was a scientist, and you can't tell me he—

DOYLE　　Yes.

PAUL　　—was murdered because of his work to promote peace, to—

DOYLE　　That's exactly what I—"promote pea—"?—no—look, back up, because, in the first— to say "scientist" is, alright, misleading, because, look, look, he, look, he didn't wear a white coat, he was "mixed up" in a dangerous—

PAUL　　He was a—

DOYLE　　—a da— according to *The New York Times*, dangerous *world*, that is the reality, that is the truth and, Paul, you can't come in here, with your, you know, pie in the—"to promote peace," which I don't under— you cannot come in here and say "these last five weeks, I've done so much."

PAUL　　But I—

DOYLE　　You cannot say, "I need to know."

PAUL　　That's—

DOYLE　　You cannot say, "I've tried every angle."

PAUL　　I *have* tri—

DOYLE　　You cannot say, "I've spoken to"—

PAUL　　I've seen—

DOYLE　　"To so many people, police," uhh, "police"—

PAUL　　Ambassa—

DOYLE   "Ambassadors, generals," without acknowledging that your father lived in a dangerous and and and volatile environment which, which, no listen, this is ger*mane*, because to assume that his death has something to do with or can be addressed somehow by the with the help of the CIA, with me, with—

PAUL   But let me—

DOYLE   No, because—

PAUL   Let me—let me—because when I called you, when I called you, you said you would, you said, "I will help you."

DOYLE   I said I would see you.

PAUL   You said—

DOYLE   Listen: I said I would, okay?, "see" you, not—

PAUL   You said—

DOYLE   Those are the, that is the word I used.

PAUL   "I will help"…

DOYLE   But look. I would not have made such a—it simply is not within my purview. I am in Operations, I, that is my job. I am a GS12, which is practically nothing. I sit here and from this little office I send and receive messages, cables, regarding the—

PAUL   Cables.

DOYLE   —activities of, yes, agents in the field—

PAUL   You send cables.

DOYLE   That is what I do, I deal with, with, with travel arrangements, financial transactions, the details of of the movements and activities of agents in the—You simply would not believe the mundanity of my position.

PAUL   You said you would help me—

DOYLE   Look. Is it not possible that, that you heard what you
               wanted to hear, that, tell me if this doesn't—because,
               and I understand this, you are on a mission,

PAUL   —You *said*—

DOYLE   and it is noble of you—he was, yes, murdered, and I
               understand how you "feel," I understand that he was,
               to you, a kind man, a gentle man, a good man, a
               "pass the peas" kind of man who never spoke of his
               work—look, let me make this point—and that work,
               the nature, Paul, of that work, was such that he could
               not even hint to his own family—

PAUL   That doesn't mean—

DOYLE   —and he is murdered, he is shot to death in a church,
               for no apparent *reason*, and yet because of certain
               factors, the fact that he was a military scientist, the—

PAUL   He was *not*—

DOYLE   —the, listen, the fact that there were no witnesses to
               his his death, facts such as these emerge, and
               somehow, out of all this, you, Paul, a
               schoolteacher—

PAUL   An assistant profess—

DOYLE   An assistant professor, from Toronto Canada, you
               who have taken it upon yourself to "seek the truth,"
               as you say, to "seek justice" for this crime, you come
               to me for "help," to the CIA for "help," and, although
               I respect your mission, though I envy you your sense
               of filial duty, though I find it touching, I am "at a
               loss" to know, okay, *why*, you would come to me,
               to, why you would attempt to solicit my help when,
               until a week ago, until I saw the newspaper reports, I
               didn't know your father from—

PAUL   "Didn't know"...?

DOYLE —I never heard of—

PAUL You "never"—

DOYLE I never—

PAUL "Never heard of..."

DOYLE Never heard of your father, never heard, therefore, of *you*, and yet you call me, you call me up, and use the name General Sparrow, to which I do, yes, respond, because, it is, to me, a "name," which yours is not, which your father's is, I'm sorry, not.

PAUL How can you—He did things for you, worked for you, my father worked for *you*, how can you just, you treat him like, you wash him—

DOYLE What are you saying, "worked for"...

PAUL —and I don't, in this moment, I do not understand why he had to die, when the things he believed in, when the things he fought for were the things *you* fought for, the things you hired him to fight for, the things—

DOYLE Would you listen? Would you listen to what you are saying, to the alleg—do you know what you are suggesting, that he was a, what, he was an agent of the CIA, do you—

PAUL I'm not suggesting, I'm saying: he was "on the payroll," he "had a deal," he, these are the things he told me, and you have, in that file, the, or in your head, the reason he was—

DOYLE This is—

PAUL The reason he was, terminated.

DOYLE Termi—

PAUL Yes.

DOYLE   Now look—

PAUL   You hired him to work on cluster bombs for "a
             friendly nation," you sent him to work for—

DOYLE   Now look—

PAUL   Sent him to work for—

DOYLE   Je*sus*—

PAUL   You authorized it, he was working for you. He told
             me. He told me the day he died he was working for
             you and I have the…

DOYLE   What. You have the what, Paul, the "proof"? The
             "proof," is that what you—Okay, you speak with, I
             believe you, the sincerity of what you're saying. So
             here's what I'm prepared to—Look. I lied to you when
             I said "I never knew"—

PAUL   I knew you were lying but I respected your right to do
             that.

DOYLE   I know, it was obvious that I was lying. You
             understood that a lie was passing between us and I,
             yes, respected you for allowing me to take my
             position. What I'll do is this. I'll tell you what I
             know, as much as I can, and if it's, but, the thing is,
             you can't, I don't want you, okay?, "using" this,
             alright, this is strictly between you and, you and…

PAUL   Okay.

DOYLE   Because I did know your father, did, very briefly, have
             the privilege of, the honour of, but, and I must say
             this, he was not "our man in"…He was someone
             who, well, I tried to help him, and I want to
             emphasize that point of "help" because I could see
             that the man meant well and that he had wedged
             himself into a, that he was desperate and I
             sympathized, greatly, with his cause. I met with him,
             once, two months—

PAUL   Once.

DOYLE   That's right, once, two months ago, as part of an investigation. Two months ago, I got a phone call from a colleague of mine, an associate from, from a country that I will identify by its cryptonym, AD.

PAUL   A, d.

DOYLE   Now this AD is what you would call a "friendly nation," a nation in which we have many interests, strategic interests, economic. Because of its particular nature, its particular history, its particular peoples, all of its particulars, AD finds itself surrounded by a number of hostile neighbours. One of these neighbours is a country which I will refer to as SI. I will keep this simple. SI is ruled by a dictator. SI is a country with which we do not permit trade, of any sort, but we are especially concerned, given the brutal, given the expansionist nature of the regime, we are concerned with military trade, and we guard with great vigilance against it. You can imagine, then, my reaction, which was of disbelief, of dismay, when the gentleman from AD—

PAUL   The friendly—

DOYLE   —called to, that's right, called to say that he had detected, by way of satellite, the occurrence of an explosion, a flash of light over a mountain in central SI.

Scene Two

> *Office of ED SPARROW, Head of Space*
> *Defense, the Pentagon: SPARROW and*
> *DOYLE.*
>
> *NOTE: From here to the end of Scene Twelve,*
> *the dialogue of characters who speak "outside" of*
> *a scene will be in italics, as it is here, where*
> *PAUL "watches" DOYLE and SPARROW.*

SPARROW   Then it wasn't a courtesy sort of call.

PAUL   *(to DOYLE, in his office) You went to see Ed Sparrow?*

DOYLE   *That is what I did. He is the Head of Space Defense at the Pentagon. This is his area. I was, I have to admit, lost in the language in which the gentleman from AD spoke—*

SPARROW   What sort of language?

DOYLE   The language of technology, General, of space defense, of "trajectories" and "missiles and, what, "signatures"—

SPARROW   Well it's a complex area, Mr. Doyle.

DOYLE   It is, sir, yes, and that is—

SPARROW   John, is it?

DOYLE   —that is—yes—and that is why—

SPARROW   What do you think of the kids, John?

DOYLE   Of the—?

SPARROW   These are my boys, John, and these are their boys.

DOYLE   Good. Yes. These *words*, General, they mean nothing to me and—

SPARROW   Have you got kids?

DOYLE   —I need to gain an understanding of the concepts, of the—

SPARROW   Have you got kids, John?

DOYLE   "Have I got"—?

SPARROW   I'm retiring in two years, John. There's gonna be a new administration, John, old wine, new bottles, same wine, John, same whining, same—

DOYLE   These *words*, General.

SPARROW   They're gonna clear me out, John. I'm old school. They've got some Harvard quarterback ready to take over for me.

DOYLE   Well you've done—

SPARROW   The man's got ivy league crawling all over him, John.

DOYLE   You've done good work, General.

SPARROW   Thank you for saying so.

DOYLE   Your record is—Thirty-five years.

SPARROW   How can I help you, John?

DOYLE I need you to help me interpret these words, General, these, not just these words, but these satellite—these were sent to me—

SPARROW Where did you get these?

DOYLE They were taken by an AD satellite in central—

SPARROW Jesus.

DOYLE General?

SPARROW It's a missile, John.

DOYLE What kind of—

SPARROW It's a Snowman missile.

DOYLE "Snowman"?

SPARROW Every shell has its own, look, its own *signature*, John, look, when it re-enters the atmosphere, its own trail of smoke, and *this* goddamn trail—where did you *get* these?

DOYLE As I said, the gentleman from AD, he'd been hearing rumours of, actually not rumours but humintel that SI was involved in space de—

SPARROW You've got spies in SI and they took this long to come forward with this information?

DOYLE I only know what—

SPARROW They waited for a goddamn test shot—Jesus Christ, John. This is, *goddamn it*—

DOYLE (to PAUL) *Just like that, very agitated, very upset, over these satellite photos.*

SPARROW Do you know a man named Donald Jackson?

DOYLE Donald—?

SPARROW   You should have a file this thick on him, him and Snowman.

DOYLE   I'll have my girl send me the files.

SPARROW   Forget the files, John, files are im*per*sonal. Shit.

DOYLE   *(to PAUL) He briefed me.*

SPARROW   I worked on Snowman for—25 years with Donald Jackson.

DOYLE   *You* did.

SPARROW   Jackson came to me in the 50s.

DOYLE   "Came to"…

SPARROW   Have you got kids, John?

DOYLE   General?

SPARROW   Children, or, what is it, are you a career man, or, what?

DOYLE   I'm not sure I see the—

SPARROW   Okay, John. Jackson came to me in 1958. It was the year after the first sputnik launch. You have to understand the *time,* the *achievement.* The Soviets had put an object into orbit. It scared the shit out of us, absolutely terrifying this stuff was, John. Now I'm a researcher at this time, this time, the late fifties, and now I'm retiring.

DOYLE   You're—

SPARROW   Never mind, John, I just saw the trajectory of my godamned life. I'm a researcher, with the space program, and part of my job is to recruit scientists to the cause, military men, civilians, what have you, I cast wide the *net.* I'm in California, at a convention. Stanford University. Huge hall. This guy gets up to speak. And he's walking the *walk*, I mean his balls are shaking the floorboards.

JACKSON   *(at convention) Testing, testing.*

SPARROW   I check the program."Donald Jackson," a Canadian. He's supposed to deliver a paper called "War in Space." Well there's maybe fifteen people sitting in the auditorium. Alright? I mean, a Canadian.

JACKSON   *Is this on?*

SPARROW   But uh, after he speaks.

JACKSON   *Is this fucking thing on?*

SPARROW   He has a vision you see.

JACKSON   *Can somebody turn this goddamn mike on?*

DOYLE   He's a visionary?

JACKSON   *Fuck the mike, I'm just gonna talk.*

SPARROW   He was the first to realize –

JACKSON   *What?*

SPARROW   – that if missiles could be used to launch attacks, –

JACKSON   *Well move closer you pencil neck.*

SPARROW   – they could also be used –

JACKSON   *Okay.*

SPARROW   – to stop them.

JACKSON   *War. I'm gonna talk today about ...what?...WHAT? Donald Jack...Donald Jackson...JACKSON... Someone, somebody told me you should always start with a uh, a, a joke. I'm with the Canadian Space Defense Council...Isn't that funny? The Canadian Space Defense Council, home of cowards, pencil necks and a thousand monkeys: rivalled in incompetency and careerism only by the self-serving shitheads in Ottawa who make up its budget. "Nuff about them. I, um, I want to thank you for inviting me to this, this conference. After listening to some of the lectures this morning, some of the papers, I think I now have a deeper appreciation of why these gatherings are called "conventions." What I mean is I'm not here to be "conventional." I didn't leave my pregnant wife in a snowstorm and fly three thousand miles to talk about the past, no. I want to talk about the future...I want to talk about the present...I want to talk about who we are and where we are and what we have to do get to where we want to be...*

I had the chance, on a recent trip to Europe, to visit the graveyards of the boys who fell in the muddy fields of World War I, and as I walked along the rows of white crosses, I couldn't help but weep. "And did those feet in Ancient Time walk upon England's Mountains green?" Those feet beneath which lay their own graves. Those feet, beneath which fell the bombs that took them forever from those they loved. The boys buried in those graves, those boys went to fight for peace; for their homes—homes they never saw again. Our homes. They went "over there," as the song says, because that is where the war was fought; well gentlemen, there is no "over there" anymore; "over there" is over here, right where we stand. The homes those boys died to protect are the new battlefields. The Russians will soon be able to obliterate us, without having to set foot on our soil. That is a fact, and I don't dispute facts, I deal with them. I put my hands around their skinny little necks and shake 'em 'til they've told me everything I need to know. And when I put my hands around the neck of a Russian missile, this is what it told me: it can be stopped, intercepted in space, the space above our cities where our sons and daughters lay sleeping. We will build thousands of long range missiles, and bury them in fields all over this country. When the Russians launch, our missiles will go up, up, into space, where they will detonate, releasing a million pieces of shrapnel, a snowstorm in space, waiting,

waiting for the Russian shells, which will hit the shrapnel, and explode, harmlessly, in the blackness...end of missile, end of threat, end of war on earth. We will fight our wars, if wars must be fought, high above us.

When my son is born—and my wife's assured me that it will be a son—I'll look at him, and know that my missile will protect him. And my missile, gentlemen, my snowstorm, will cost a tenth, a tenth of what it will cost this nation to defend itself from attack using the systems now being considered by the Pentagon.

SPARROW I'm taken by Donald Jackson's vision. I pour everything I've got into this vision. Twenty-five years I pour, because I'm *loyal* to the man, he in*spires* my loyalty, through his *words*, alright, which I accept as articles of *faith*. I want Snowman to work. We become, I wouldn't say good friends, but more than colleagues. I mean the man is one part this, one part that. But he is unstable...

DOYLE *(to PAUL) This is his* view.

SPARROW Things aren't going well, the calculations aren't making sense, the tests are proving fruitless, he tells me he doesn't know how long he can *take* it, this kind of talk, alright. After twenty-five years of this, waiting, failed tests, further study, no signs of progress, just words, promises, tomorrows, states of depression, I have to—

DOYLE *(to PAUL) This is what was said to me.*

SPARROW I have to cancel the project. I remember the day I told him. It was raining outside, a grim gray fucking morning.

JACKSON *What are you telling me, Ed?*

SPARROW *I can't defend you anymore, Don. You have made promises, for twenty years and more you have promised to deliver a system that would render us infallible against attack.*

JACKSON   *That's exactly what I'm going to give you.*

SPARROW   *When?*

JACKSON   *You can't put a goddamn time limit on this.*

SPARROW   *I'm doing you a favour, Don. I'm telling you, Snowman does not work.*

JACKSON   *The fuck you talking about, "does not"—*

SPARROW   *I am talking about time moving faster than ideas, your ideas, Don. Twenty-five years ago Snowman made sense. Now it doesn't. We ran it through the computer. It won't fly.*

JACKSON   *What are you telling me?*

SPARROW   *We're looking at lasers in space, not missiles. We're switching our research.*

JACKSON   *Strategic Defense Initiative.*

SPARROW   *Don—*

JACKSON   *S, D, fuckin I. You think I don't hear things? I've made some calls. I've got people telling me things.*

SPARROW   *Don, don't—*

JACKSON   *I've got people....oh Jesus. Twenty-five years, Ed? You're gonna fuckin destroy me.*

SPARROW   *Snowman is no longer viable.*

JACKSON   *"No longer viable."*

SPARROW   *I mean it was a lofty idea, Don, but time—*

JACKSON   *"Lofty i"—I mean where did you learn to talk like this?*

SPARROW   *Talk's got nothing to do with it.*

JACKSON *What the fuck happened to you?*

SPARROW *This doesn't mean you're out.*

JACKSON *You were a scientist.*

SPARROW *We want your work, Don.*

JACKSON *Now you're a bur-eau-crat, a servant of the state, a servant of paper, of words, you bow to the fucking gods in the White House.*

SPARROW *I've been ordered to pour everything I've got into SDI.*

JACKSON *You know SDI's bullshit, "Star Wars" science fiction...*

SPARROW *This isn't about science. It's about economics. We're going to make the Soviets match us dollar-for-dollar. We're going to bankrupt them. I want you to be a part of it.*

JACKSON *What is that, your penance, your pity, fuck you and your "lofty ideas" talk, send me a memo."We ran it through the computer," bullshit, you ran it through your mind, your conventional little mind, you can't see what I can see, nobody can, I can see it, it will "fly" it is "viable" it is possible you fuck it will fly it will fly.*

SPARROW He began offering Snowman to anyone who'd take it, any nation, first or third world, it didn't matter to him. That made him dangerous, unstable. I was forced to prevent him from acquiring any contracts with nations seeking our military assistance.

DOYLE *(to PAUL) He blackballed him.*

PAUL *He said Snowman didn't work, he told you that. Why would he keep my father from selling it?*

SPARROW Because when I realized what might happen—

DOYLE *He grabbed some pencils from his desk.*

SPARROW   Let's take the present scenario. The pencil holder is
AD; the pencils, AD missiles. The picture of the kids
are the people of SI. Jackson convinces the kids that
he can make them invulnerable, as though he were
putting his hand over them, as though his hand were
impenetrable. The kids shoot at the pencil holder. The
pencil holder, having nothing to lose, fires pencils at
the kids. Some hit the hand; some get through. You
see what I'm saying? You'll need to have a word with
Donald Jackson.

DOYLE   I'll have my girl arrange a briefing. I'd like you to
take in the meeting, General, in the event he uses
language I might not understand.

SPARROW   I don't know if I can, John. This history between us.
I don't know that being in the room with him—

DOYLE   I don't want you *in* the room.

Scene Three

DOYLE's office: DOYLE and JACKSON.

JACKSON   (*looking at satellite photo*) This is Snowman. This is a test shot of the Snowman missile. And very soon now, very soon now, we will announce the creation—

DOYLE   "We"?

JACKSON   My people.

DOYLE   Your—?

JACKSON   The people I'm working for, and I, will announce the details of a space defense system, created by me, using technology that was available to the United States.

DOYLE   ...And it has been completed?

JACKSON   Very soon now is what I said, and "very soon now" is what I am saying.

DOYLE   *He got up to leave—*

JACKSON   Is that all? Because my wife is waiting for me outside...

DOYLE   Please, if you don't—just, a word, really.

JACKSON A word.

DOYLE That's right—Dr. Jackson, I have to make it clear to you what you may be predicating with your work on—

JACKSON What do you want, Mr. Doyle?

DOYLE I want to help you.

JACKSON You want to do what?

DOYLE Let me be candid. I read the files, sir. When Snowman was cancelled, when you threatened to take your research elsewhere, the Pentagon took steps to—

JACKSON Ed Sparrow "took steps".

DOYLE Took steps to have you discredited, villified, worse than—and yet I had no reason, sir, no reason to disbelieve the veracity of the opinions against your favour. And then an extraordinary thing happened, Dr. Jackson. In my meeting with General Sparrow, as he recounted his history with you, I sat in amazement as I listened to the words you spoke, of "survival" of "protection," these words touched me, sir, moved me sir, through the distortions of memory and another person's voice, and yet, your vision, sir, your vision shone through.

JACKSON I see.

DOYLE And when you spoke of graveyards, sir, of "the boys" going to die "over there" I could barely contain my, my, emotion. You spoke of loss, sir, of remorse for that which is gone, of the unbearable grip which the dead hold on our minds, and I thought, sir, of my brother, my brother who died in the jungles of Vietnam, sir, fell in the jungles of Vietnam beneath the feet of his friends.

JACKSON I'm sorry, John, I—

DOYLE
My brother went to—and this is a picture of us as children, as boys, I keep it on my desk as a— challenge—a reminder, that he went to Vietnam for the same reason I joined the Agency, "to perform," as it is written in our charter, "to perform such functions and duties affecting the national security as may be, from time to time, required," as was his time, as is my time. Because we both believe, believed, in protecting the idea that is this country. We understood that there are different ways in which to do that. My father did not understand that, Dr. Jackson, never spoke to me after my brother's death, as though somehow, I failed to protect my own brother, as though I should have been alongside him as he bled to death, as though somehow I would not have wanted to be there, to comfort him, you see, to— Now I look at you and I say, *you* wanted to protect us, and yet, and yet you were driven away from us. The time has now come for you to return, and I want to honour the memory of my brother by—

JACKSON
To return?

DOYLE
Do you understand?

JACKSON
Return to what?

DOYLE
To the Pentagon, to work...

JACKSON
The Pentagon? To *what?* Work for Ed Sparrow?

DOYLE
I want you to live amongst us again, to cease your present activities.

JACKSON
To what—?

DOYLE
Listen, cease your present activi—

JACKSON
Cease my present—?

DOYLE
The people of SI are not your people, Dr. Jackson: we are your people.

JACKSON
You son of a bitch.

DOYLE   They have taken your ideas and used them to pursue a policy of aggression and and, it may be, genocide, and you have allowed yourself to be used by them, Dr. Jackson, in order to, what, to pay back General Sparrow for what he did to you?

JACKSON   You prick...

DOYLE   Dr. Jackson...

JACKSON   You goddamn prick...

DOYLE   I understand your wanting revenge for—

JACKSON   You goddamn pencil-necked little shit.

DOYLE   Would you listen to—

JACKSON   Who the fuck are you to talk to me?

DOYLE   Paul, he wouldn't let me speak.

JACKSON   You think you know the inside of me? Answer me— who the *fuck* are you?

DOYLE   I'm trying to help, help you.

JACKSON   Help me? Fuck your help, fuck your snot-nosed condescending airs. I *worked* for this, I *gave things up* for this, I've—

DOYLE   I understand—

JACKSON   I have struggled, I *have*, all my life, and if I hadn't been betrayed, if this fucking country had appreciated what I tried to do for it, the way my people appreciate—listen to me, I'll tell you about who my people are, alright, and don't you talk to me about allegiance, because I owe allegiance to anybody whose vision of this world corresponds to my own, a world of peace, of, yes, peace, through deterrence, and nobody else was willing to give me the chance, *a* chance, to do what it is I—

DOYLE   This is what I'm saying, I *want to give you*—

JACKSON   Do you hear me?

DOYLE   I do, and I am telling you, I am telling you that it is
            in your own best interest to consider what it is I—
            because there are people, Dr. Jackson, who— There
            are people who are "concerned" that, that what you are
            providing SI is not, is not what you *say*, but—

JACKSON   It *is* what I say, what people? Ed Sparrow? *Fuck* Ed
            Sparrow.

DOYLE   There are people, Dr. Jackson, who *will*, if you
            continue your present work, who will—the people of
            AD are a brusque people, and I have no doubt that
            they would attempt, through intimidation or, or,
            intimidation, to have you stop your work on
            Snowman.

JACKSON   I can't stop my work.

DOYLE   I am offering—

JACKSON   I *can't*. Tell your "people," tell them there are still
            men left in this world who believe in what they're
            doing, who believe that what they're doing is *right*,
            and *good,* and *moral.*

DOYLE   Moral?

JACKSON   That's right, and I know that word doesn't appear in
            your *lexicon.*

DOYLE   Morality—is that what you think this is about?

JACKSON   It is, because I believe in the—

DOYLE   Forget "morality," forget "right," forget "wrong," this
            isn't about—this is about facts, the who and the
            what and the when and let the morality take care of
            itself, because in the jungle there is no morality, in
            the fields there is no morality, there's you and your
            tribe running naked and a watering hole and a piece of

land and tonight's dinner, there's another tribe, also naked, and they want to drink at your watering hole, they want to live by your watering hole, only there's not enough for them, there's not enough land for them, there's not enough water for them, but they want it, they want what you've got, and you've got three options: run from them, fight with them, embrace them, and this is not "morality," this is survival, this is—they don't care about what you "say" you are doing, what you "think" you are doing, all they see is *this*, *these*, your hands and what you are doing with them, forget the rest, forget the Things Thought, forget the Things Said: all that matters, truly matters, are the Things Done, Done, to survive. And that tribe over there, that tribe in the distance, that tribe approaching your watering hole, they want to know, what is this thing you are doing…

JACKSON   Well you tell your "tribe"…tell them to watch the skies, because very soon now, very soon now they will see me there, they will see "this thing I am doing," and they will say, if they have words, "this *thing* could have been ours."

DOYLE   Please…

JACKSON   Tell them to ff—…tell them I've got nothing to lose.

DOYLE   Are you looking for the bullet? Are you looking for—? You don't have to answer.

Scene Four

DOYLE's office: DOYLE and PAUL.

PAUL   And he, what, he just walked?

DOYLE   He, yes—

PAUL   Just turned you down...

DOYLE   Exactly, he "just walked," because, would a rational person, having heard—

PAUL   And everything you told me is everything you told my father?

DOYLE   Yes. After that, the gentleman from AD took over, it was, I presume, his call. I had no idea he would deal with your father in such a, such a brusque manner, if indeed it was the gentleman from AD who, who made this decision, which is something which I cannot know, something which—look. I was asked to speak with your father: I didn't *have* to offer him a deal. I *offered*. I *warned*. I *implored*. He *walked*. I told you, I could see he was looking for the bullet.

PAUL   What does that, I don't know what that *means*.

DOYLE   You know what it means, he *wanted* them to come after him, I could see that, the man had had enough, he could—

PAUL   What?

DOYLE   Exactly—

PAUL   You are saying that my father wanted to die?

DOYLE   That is my conclusion.

PAUL   You are saying. Alright. You are saying you had a
              phone call from a "gentleman from AD," that *you* had
              a phone call.

DOYLE   Yes…

PAUL   You are saying that you went to see Ed Sparrow. You
              are saying that you met with my father *once*.

DOYLE   That is what I am saying.

PAUL   And I am saying this:

ANNA   *Paul?*

PAUL   I had a call.

DOYLE   You had a call?

ANNA   *I need to see you.*

PAUL   From my mother. Six weeks ago.

Scene Five

ANNA JACKSON's home in Toronto. ANNA and PAUL.

ANNA   Paul, I don't know what to do, I don't know what to *do.* Your father, your father's in trouble, he needs, needs to see you.

PAUL   To see *me?*

ANNA   He's in trouble, Paul, terrible…

PAUL   "Trouble," what…?

ANNA   I don't know, just that—

PAUL   What, is he home? Where is he?

ANNA   He's in Europe.

PAUL   *Europe?*

ANNA   He needs to—

PAUL   He's in Europe, and he needs to see me?

ANNA   Yes.

PAUL   I can't go to Europe. I've got a class in…I've got to *teach,* I can't just go to Europe and…I've got Katie this weekend.

ANNA   No, I…I called Susan, she said she'd make other arrange—

PAUL   You called Susan? What is this? What is going *on?*

ANNA   He's working on Snowman again.

DOYLE   *You knew nothing of this?*

PAUL   *No.*

ANNA   He flew home last week. I hadn't seen him in months, months, he's hardly been home. He said he had a meeting in Washington and would I drive him? "We'll make a vacation out of it," he said. He *asked* me to drive him, do you see? I didn't *know,* how could I know?

PAUL   Alright, al*right,* just, just…

ANNA   I drove, he sat in the back. He was afraid, I could see that he was terribly afraid, and I wanted, wanted to know, but he wouldn't wouldn't *talk* to me. The whole trip, just *silence* until we got, got close to Washington. Then he told me, he said he had to see "some guy," that's all, "some guy" at the CIA.

DOYLE   *I have not denied meeting with your father. I mean if that's the point of your—*

ANNA   I should have turned the car around, Pauly, just *turned* and kept driving, driven off the end of the world and not stopped because I knew, I *knew* when he said what he was saying and it was "I lied to you, I *lied* to you, my words mean nothing, my pledges, *nothing.*"

PAUL   Lied?

ANNA He promised me, you don't know what it *took*, to get him to promise me, to have nothing more to do with the Americans, after what they did to him, what Ed Sparrow did to him, forced us to run, hide from the world, from the fool the world believed he was, even you, Paul, believed he was.

PAUL I did not believe.

JACKSON *You don't believe what they say in the papers, Pauly?*

PAUL *I'm not saying that.*

JACKSON *This is Sparrow talking. Listen, "a highly placed source at the Pentagon"—now who do you think that is?—"at the Pentagon has revealed that tests were rigged in order to convince Congress of the efficacy of the Snowman Missile System." Sparrow's doing this to me, Pauly: he knows I can sell Snowman.*

ANNA *He's afraid of your father.*

JACKSON *Anna...*

PAUL *It says in the article you knew Snowman would never work. Is that true?*

JACKSON *Pauly...*

PAUL *Is it? It says you took kick-backs. Did you?*

ANNA *How can you ask these—*

PAUL *It says you lied to Congress. Did you?*

ANNA *They want people to think—*

JACKSON *Please...*

ANNA *He's a traitor, don't you see that?*

JACKSON *I think I know how to talk.*

ANNA *You said you wanted me to be here.*

PAUL   *Jesus.*

JACKSON   *That doesn't mean you speak for me.*

PAUL   *I'm going.*

JACKSON   *Pauly, Pauly, listen to me. This is what happens. A man offers his people a way to the future and, there's a lesson here, Pauly, if you'll listen—because the people who hold the power, they're afraid, afraid of this new way, because if this new way comes about, they won't hold the power anymore. I'm being sacrificed, Pauly, because I won't play along. You know that, don't you? Do you think I'm a fool, Paul?*

PAUL   *I don't know who you are. Tell me who you are. I used to tell myself, it's alright if he's hardly home. He goes to work in the United States, the Pentagon, he's an important man, doing important work. For the good. What am I supposed to tell myself now? I remember once, when you were home, once, and we looked at the stars together. You said, "There's Cassiopeia," and I said "Where? Where? I don't see it." I started to cry because I couldn't see it, and you said "Look hard, harder, you have to look hard and you'll see it." Now I'm looking. I'm looking very hard."*

ANNA   And did you? Did you look hard? Did you even think of us when we went to Europe? Did you try to imagine what it was I went through with him? His misery and self-pity, the booze and the screaming and the crying fits and night sweats, the feelings of failure and betrayal, the mood swings, the smashing of walls and glasses and plates. And the waiting, waiting by the phone, waiting for the day when the phone would ring and a voice on the other end would say, "Come back. You may come back now." But there was no call. We went on walks in graveyards, the way we did when we were young. And like then, he would run his hands along the crosses and cry real tears for the boys who had died. For us.

PAUL   Why did you stay with him?

ANNA   Because he's my husband. He read poetry again, Paul, your father. Yes, he even wrote some. After a year of running, when we finally settled in a little apartment in France, and spent our days in cafés, taking long walks and talking endlessly about our lives, what they might have been and what they might become, when I begged him to give up his work and be at peace with himself, to be at peace, I felt, I felt we had finally begun to have the life that was promised me. Then. The phone rang. And he was working again, flying around the world and I made him swear to me that he would *never* work for the Americans, made him swear that he would never let anyone bring him to his knees again. And he swore. I came back to Toronto, and I never knew, *never knew* about his work, Paul, you have to believe that, not until he told me, in the car, about his meeting at the CIA.

DOYLE   *This is absurd, Paul, what am I supposed to understand from—*

ANNA   Do you under*stand?* When we got to the CIA, when he got out of the car, he, he crossed himself—

PAUL   What?

ANNA   Just, like this, very—carefully. I went to the hotel and waited. I waited a long time. When he came into the room, I could…his face was in his hands and he was in tears, crawling, crawling to where I lay on the bed, and I could barely hear him but I heard him. "Tell me who I am," he said.

PAUL   "Tell me"?

ANNA   "You are my husband." "I need to see the boys," he said. "I need to see the boys, if only I could speak with the boys, explain to them, make amends." In the morning, he was gone. I know where he is, Paul. You have to come with me, to talk to him, to…

PAUL   Jesus, I'm late, I'm *missing* it now.

ANNA You have to come with me. He's done so much for you, given up so much for—

PAUL What do you want from me?

ANNA Your heart. Where is it? Why do you hide it? He needs you.

PAUL What can I say to him?

ANNA Put your arms around him. Drag him home, if that's what it takes.

PAUL Home? To what? His life is his *work,* bring him home to *what?*

ANNA Nothing.

PAUL Tell me. What will he do here?

ANNA "Nothing" is what he will do. Nothing.

Scene Six

DOYLE's office: DOYLE and PAUL.

DOYLE   You see what I'm saying.

PAUL   What you're…?

DOYLE   There was nothing that could have been done, even said, it was the man's nature, and nature cannot be—

PAUL   *No.* We went to Europe and we con*fronted* him and. (*cutting himself off*) The things you said—

DOYLE   Yes.

PAUL   *Everything you've said.*

DOYLE   Everything I've—

PAUL   A lie passed between us.

Scene Seven

A graveyard: JACKSON, digging up earth,
ANNA and PAUL.

ANNA   What are you doing?

JACKSON   I'm so glad to see you, Paul…

DOYLE   *Paul? What are you telling me?*

PAUL   *We found him in a graveyard.*

JACKSON   …come here, Paul, tell me, I need you to tell me
                something…

ANNA   Donald, please get up.

JACKSON   "And did those feet…," you know what that is? "…in
                ancient time, walk upon England's…" Paul, you
                know what that is? *Paul.*

PAUL   It's a poem.

JACKSON   I couldn't remember it all. I thought if I came here, I'd
                remember it all. You know it, Paul.

PAUL   No…

ANNA   Donald…

JACKSON   "And was the Holy Lamb of God"...

ANNA   Donald...

JACKSON   What is it, what is it, "Lamb of God..." Paul I used to sing it to you, Anna tell him how I used to sing it, "in the good old days," eh Anna, sitting on my, "and was the Holy Lamb of God in England's pleasant pastures," yes, "seen?" Come on come on you know it.

ANNA   Stop it, Donald.

JACKSON   What's the next line?

PAUL   I don't remember.

JACKSON   You remember, you remember, we used to get it wrong, because we thought, remember, we thought it was "continents divide," "and did the continents divide"... remember, and it didn't make any sense but we sang it anyway, and, come on, Paul, "And did the Countenance Divine shine forth upon our"—goddamn it, Paul, help me.

PAUL   I don't remember the—

ANNA   Donald, I want you to—

JACKSON   Goddammit, Anna, I'm trying to remember the poem, I came here to sing the praises of these boys, these, they fell beneath their feet my guns and bullets fell beneath their feet...

ANNA   Paul...

PAUL   "Upon our crowded hill"...

JACKSON   "Upon our crowded," that's it, "crowded hill, and was Jerusalem"...that isn't it, what's the matter with you, "crowded," it's "clouded," *clouded*"...

PAUL   "Clouded hills"...

JACKSON   Can't you remember a simple poem, a simple line of
               poetry, what's the matter with you?

PAUL   I'm trying…

JACKSON   Help me, help me, Paul, help me, "Bring me my
               sword of burning gold"… it's coming back to
               me…help me sing to them, help me dig them up,
               help me put them back together, we just need a little
               flesh, "bring me my arrows of desire"…we'll put
               them back together they'll walk again it's fine you'll
               see, they didn't die they just fell beneath their feet I
               didn't mean to send them away I only wanted to
               protect them protect them from ourselves our…

ANNA   Donald, tell him—

JACKSON   This is what I've done this is me here in the mud and
               dirt and bones and dust of the young and innocent and
               brave and STUPID…what did they think they were
               doing marching to the tune of time or somebody's red
               flag into the wind of "I shall not cease from mental
               fight, nor shall my" goddamn it goddamn it
               PAAAAUUUL…

ANNA   Donald, tell him. Tell him what you told me, in the
               hotel room, Donald, what you told me about your
               meeting.

JACKSON   …We had a deal, Paul.

PAUL   …Who?…

JACKSON   Doyle. To protect, to offer peace, to—we had a deal,
               we had a deal.

Scene Eight

DOYLE's office: DOYLE and JACKSON.

DOYLE   That's right, "we do for you, you do for us," that is the deal, except for *this*, the thing *you* were supposed to do, the terms of that thing have, from what I hear, changed.

JACKSON   "Changed," I don't under—

DOYLE   I had a visit from Ed Sparrow.

JACKSON   Ed Sparrow?

DOYLE   That's right, he came to see me, in a state of—

DOYLE   *(to Paul:) Just a second.*

PAUL   *"A state of, what, panic"—*

DOYLE   *What are you saying?*

PAUL   *What my father told me, in that graveyard, told me, about your meeting.*

DOYLE   A state of, what, panic, no, agitation, no, he had a fucking apoplexy on me.

Scene Nine

DOYLE's office: DOYLE and SPARROW.

SPARROW We have a problem, Mr. Doyle.

DOYLE Which is what?

SPARROW Do you know a man named Donald Jackson?

DOYLE Donald—?

SPARROW Jackson. There's a rumour he's working for you.

DOYLE For me?

SPARROW There's a rumour you've got him working on a space defense program for—

DOYLE *(to Paul:) This is absurd—what is this?*

PAUL *What you said. Sparrow came to see you.*

SPARROW I had a call this morning from a colleague of mine in AD, a very brusque man who sent me these satellite photos.

DOYLE *The photos were sent to—*

SPARROW The signature of this missile describes a trajectory that—

DOYLE   "Signature"?

SPARROW   —that belongs to—

DOYLE   I'm sorry, General, these *words* —this *language*—

SPARROW   Every missile has its own trail of smoke, Mr. Doyle,
             its own *sig*—

DOYLE   This is not at all—

*PAUL   This is what happened. Sparrow explained the history
             of the program, how he hired my father, fired my
             father, the twenty-five years they worked together, the
             tests, the treaties—*

SPARROW   Are these your kids?

PAUL   —the pencils—

SPARROW   Some hit the hand, some hit the kids. Do you see
             what I'm saying?

DOYLE   Jesus.

SPARROW   Do you understand now?

DOYLE   I do, General, and let me admit that the rumour is
             true, partly, that Donald Jackson is working for me,
             and I apologize for allowing that little lie to pass
             between us, but you must understand, I feel
             somewhat protective of—he was the first man I
             recruited, years a—

SPARROW   Recruited for what?

DOYLE   To work as a consultant on—as an adviser on various
             paramilitiary operations throughout the—to put out
             fires—but as to this "space defense"—"Snowman?"—
             I had no i—

SPARROW   You should have a file this thick on Jackson, him and
             Snowman.

DOYLE   It never occured to me to—

SPARROW   I'm retiring in two years, Mr. Doyle. I have no
               intention of leaving this as my *legacy*.

DOYLE   I will have a word with—

SPARROW   You'd better do more than "have a word with—" This
               is your area. You have some vague notions about the
               history of the region, the tensions in the region.

DOYLE   I do, of course.

SPARROW   Then you understand that if Jackson is giving
               Snowman to SI—

DOYLE   I hear you, and if he is working on Snowman—

SPARROW   There is no question.

DOYLE   If he is, if he's fuckin lied to me—

DOYLE   *(to Paul:) Paul, this conversation is a complete—*

PAUL   *Would you let me—*

DOYLE   *I mean I just don't speak this way, this, the vulgarity
               of, the manner of—*

PAUL   *"I'm gonna ri"—*

DOYLE   (*to SPARROW*) rip his fuckin heart out. Leave me
               the, can you leave the satellite photos with me?
               (*picking up the telephone*) I'm gonna haul his fuckin
               ass—(into phone) I want Donald Jackson here a.s.—
               cryptonym SI, RANGER—I want him here a.s.a.
               fuckin p.—I don't —I don't give a fuck what you're
               doing, you stop doing what it is you're doing hand get
               Donald Jackson on a fuckin plane.

Scene Ten

DOYLE's office: DOYLE and JACKSON.

JACKSON   What do you want from me?

DOYLE   The truth. I want to show you something. I want you to see this because I respect you and I don't want to put you in the position of having to deceive me. *(shows JACKSON the satellite photos)* I want you to tell me, because we have been very honest and truthful from Day One with each other, and I want to hear it from your own voice what this is. Tell me. Tell me what this—

JACKSON   This is Snowman.

DOYLE   Alright then.

JACKSON   It's a test shot of the Snowman missile.

DOYLE   Okay. Alright. Alright, that's— What are you doing? What the fuck do you think you're—

JACKSON   My wife's outside, she's—I told her—

DOYLE   Sit down.

JACKSON   I told her I'd just be a minute, it's raining, she's—

DOYLE   Sit down. "It's a test shot of the"—Okay. Okay. *Now.*

JACKSON   They offered me…

DOYLE   What?

JACKSON   We started talking, some General—

DOYLE   Skip the fucking details.

JACKSON   I was going to tell you, John. I was. John—

DOYLE   How close are you to deploying—

JACKSON   John, all my life I've been waiting for the time when, waiting for someone to give me the chance to—

DOYLE   How close?

JACKSON   Soon…

DOYLE   Soon when, what, when?

JACKSON   "Soon" is all we've discussed and—

DOYLE   "We"?

JACKSON   My people.

DOYLE   Your *people,* Don? Your "peop"—Who are they, your "people"? The fucking people you're giving Snowman to? Are they your "people" now? Is that what you're— talk to me—

JACKSON   Yes, because nobody else was willing to give me the chance to, a chance to—

DOYLE   Who picked you up? Who held out his hand and picked you up when you were crawling in the dirt?

JACKSON   You did, John, you did, but…

DOYLE   But—

JACKSON   John…I want to thank you, John, for what you've done for me, for helping me to regain a piece of myself, a piece of my dignity, enough for me to know that I have to finish my work—

DOYLE   Finish your work? Your work is fi—Are you listening to—Listen to this: if you do not agree to "cease and desist" your present activities—

JACKSON   You can't ask—

DOYLE   Listen, your present activities, I will need to "take steps" to ensure that your work is left uncompleted, do you understand? …Do you understand that we will come after you? Do you understand that we will come after your wife? After your children, your children's children, everything that is—

JACKSON   I can't stop my work…

DOYLE   Are you deaf?

JACKSON   I can't. You do what you have to do, I'll do what I have to. I've got nothing to lose now. Nobody gave me a chance, and these people, and they deserve as much, and they need as much, to be protected from their enemies, to be…

DOYLE   To be protected…?

JACKSON   To be, yes, protected, and that is what I am giving them, a system of defense, a system that will allow them to live in peace and, in the knowledge that their children, and, yes—

DOYLE   "A system of defense," is that what you think this is?

JACKSON   That is what I'm giving them.

DOYLE   They want your system of defense so that they can attack, so that they can launch—

JACKSON   What are you talking—

DOYLE   I'm talking about what I know: you are giving SI, your "people" a "space shield," and once your people have this "space shield" in place, they are going to go on the attack, they are going to burn—they are going to incinerate AD.

JACKSON   No, that isn't—

DOYLE   Open your, "that isn't" what?

JACKSON   "For defensive purposes only," that is what we discussed, that is what—

DOYLE   "Defensive purposes" bullshit. Open your fucking eyes and look at what it is you are.

JACKSON   I was told, "we want deterrence"…

DOYLE   You make weapons.

JACKSON   Weapons of peace, of peace, I've always believed that my inten—to offer protection to…

DOYLE   "Peace," "protection," forget those words, nobody wants these words from you: we want weapons from you, we want you to make us strong, we want you to say "there will be deaths because there must be deaths" and accept that, accept that that is what you do. We are at war, at war with every living thing in this world, everything outside of us and everything inside of us, it is who we are, and we must embrace it, embrace it and accept it, not run from it, not fight it, the one thing we must not fight but embrace. You, you fuck, open your eyes, tell me who you are, "scientist," go on, tell me, what the fuck happened to you, when did you get your notions of purity and decency, where is the white fucking coat that places you above us, what happens, what, how do you turn, how does your mind hide from you, because you live in numbers and "e" equals this, squared by that and words we don't understand, you don't live in the real—I just said to you, you fuck you fuck, you stupid, I said to you, "we will come after you" and we will and "we will come after your wife" "we will come after your children, and your children's children."...Donald. Are you looking for the bullet? Are you look—answer me, because we will put a bullet, we will put bullets into your brain, and down your spine to ensure that—The arrogance, the the the tenacity, okay, I wanted to help you, I wanted to pick you up from the shitheap Ed Sparrow threw you onto, because I could see what had been done to you, you had been stripped naked and sent away from us, I held out my hand and you took it, and I regarded you, yes, in the way of a father, you let me pick you up and now, now you want to push me away, throw me into the shit, and I am saying to you, I am telling you get back down on the ground, get back into the mud and filth, I want to see you crawl on your belly, you fuck, get down there, get the fuck down there and crawl, crawl on your belly and listen to me call that fucking asshole from AD and say:

Scene Eleven

Transition from Scene Ten. The graveyard:
JACKSON, ANNA and PAUL.

JACKSON   "Go, it's a Go, you do what you have to, go after him, because he's a scientist who will not listen to reason." And I did, I sat there and watched and didn't say a word.

PAUL   Is that what he said?

JACKSON   Not one word.

PAUL   "Come after us," is that—

JACKSON   Leave me alone, leave me alone with these boys—

PAUL   Is that what "this guy" said? "Your children's children"?

JACKSON   Go home.

ANNA   Not without you, Donald, *no*.

JACKSON   I came here to, to do, to…

ANNA   We came for you…

JACKSON   To bury my work next to them—I owe them at least that…

ANNA   We came to you knowing the risk.

JACKSON   …To wrap my work around their bones…

PAUL   *Knowing?*

ANNA   Yes, knowing.

JACKSON   …protect their shivering bones from the cold…

PAUL   He *told* you this man threatened to—

JACKSON   …from the cold down there.

PAUL   —I have to call Susan—

ANNA   It's alright, Paul. I called her. I told her to take Katie and leave the city. They're alright, they're both—

PAUL   You lied to me.

ANNA   To get you to come with me.

PAUL   I have to call—

ANNA   You *don't*, what you have to do is here, right now. I need you, I need you now, to talk to this man, to— oh, god, you're cold, you're cold and unfeeling.

JACKSON   I can hear them, whispering, and I want to say, to these boys, forgive me, forgive me.

ANNA   You don't need to make amends, Donald, not with these boys, not *these* boys. This boy.

JACKSON   Everything I did, Pauly, I did for you.

PAUL   For me…

JACKSON   I used to hold you in my arms, ask myself, "How will I protect him"? …I wanted to make it snow in space, Pauly, to protect you from the cold.

PAUL Protect me from the—*cold?* Is that what you—is that what you think you're doing? Is that what you think you've *done?* Get up. Get *up.*

ANNA Don't do this, Paul.

PAUL You asked me to come with you and I've come with you. You want me to talk to this man, let me *talk.*

ANNA Not like this, not like this…

PAUL *This* is all that's left. Did you hear what Doyle *said* to you? There are *men* who will "come after us." Did you hear him? Did his words mean anything? Or did you think only of your*self?* What did he say? What did he say to you? "We will come after your *children,"* and what did that *mean* to you? "And we will come after your *wife,"* and what did you *hear?* "And we will come after your children's children?" And what did you say? What did you *do? Nothing.* Where were your lofty ideas about "peace" and "protection," *nowhere,* because you're willing to sacrifice us, sacrifice all of us, *your wife,* this woman who—and your own *children,* the same children you used to justify your—you didn't *hear,* you did nothing, just as long as it gives you another day, another hour, another second for your what your work your work your "desire to protect?" Fuck you and all your words and all your ideas and your blindness and you get up, get up out of the—*I'd kill you myself if I thought it meant Katie would be safe, do you hear me, I'd take a gun and—I'd put my hands around your throat and never let…oh Jesus, Jesus…*Is this how you were going to protect me? You're old, you're old and feeble and…everything you've ever stood for, everything you've ever—it's nothing. Get up. Get *up.* Look at me. Your *son.* Here I am. Protect me, father. Protect me from the cold.

JACKSON Give me your hand Paul. I just want…

PAUL What.

JACKSON Peace.…

PAUL   Yes.

JACKSON   Will you help me find it?…*(crossing himself)* In the
              name of the father, the son and the holy ghost, amen.
              Anna, I want to go, I want to make, I need to make,
              my confession…

ANNA   I'll come with you.

JACKSON   No, Anna. Alone. Give me your hand Paul. It's been
              so long, Pauly, since I held you…I never want to let
              you go…There's so much I need to make up for…and
              I will…so much you need to know…and you'll
              know…this mind, Pauly, contains so much, so much
              I should have shared with you…this heart, this heart,
              so filled with lies, exploding into a thousand
              pieces…I am sorry. I know you won't say it, I know
              the words won't come, but I want to start, here, to
              help you find the words, to say, to forgive me. Will
              you help me?

PAUL   …What can I…?

JACKSON   This bag, Paul, this bag has the designs for
              Snowman. Will you take it? Will you burn it,
              destroy it? Will you do this for me, so that we can
              begin, right now—will you…?

Scene Twelve

DOYLE's office: DOYLE and PAUL.

DOYLE   You let him go.

PAUL   He said he wanted to go.

DOYLE   And you—knowing as you did that—*knowing*—

PAUL   You weren't there.

DOYLE   He was your father, and you couldn't *tell*—

PAUL   He said he wanted to come back to us, to come back—

DOYLE   To "nothing"?

ANNA   *Pauly...*

DOYLE   ...I have, in my file...the report...

ANNA   *Something I didn't tell you...*

DOYLE   ...the report which the gentleman from AD sent following the culmination of the program...

ANNA   *...after your father met with John Doyle...*

DOYLE   ...There were two agents waiting at the graveyard...

ANNA   *...when your father came to me...*

DOYLE   ...when you and your mother arrived...

ANNA   *...in the hotel room...*

DOYLE   They observed him "crawling among the graves"...

ANNA   *...on his hands and knees...*

DOYLE   When your father left you...

ANNA   *...crawling...*

DOYLE   the agents followed him.

ANNA   *...crying...*

DOYLE   They followed him into a church.

ANNA   *...and when I saw him like that...*

DOYLE   They made no attempt to hide themselves from view.

ANNA   *...there was a part of me...*

DOYLE   Your father entered the confession box.

ANNA   *...a part of me I didn't know I had...*

DOYLE   He left the confessional and "walked to where we sat"—

ANNA   *...a part of me that was glad...*

DOYLE   I am quoting directly from the—

ANNA   *...glad to see him on his hands and knees...*

DOYLE   "He attempted to make eye contact."

ANNA   *...a part of me that was thinking:*

DOYLE   He turned his back to us and knelt."

ANNA   *...forgive me for this...*

DOYLE   The agents stood and fired.

ANNA   *...it's finished...*

DOYLE   The first bullet went through his skull...

ANNA   *...it's over...*

DOYLE   ...entered his brain, exited through his forehead. Would you like me to continue?...

ANNA   *...it's over...*

DOYLE   The force of the first bullet knocked your father to the floor.

ANNA   *...the man you were is dead...*

DOYLE   He lay there, probably dead already.

ANNA   *...the man I loved will come back to me...*

DOYLE   The agents stepped forward and fired again.

ANNA   *...I might get you back now...*

DOYLE   The second shot went into his back.

ANNA   *...I won't be alone...*

DOYLE   Two more shots were fired into his spine...

ANNA   *...you won't leave me alone...*

DOYLE   ...a fifth into the head...

ANNA   *...you've left me alone...*

DOYLE   ...up close, to be sure.

ANNA   *They took this man from me, Pauly. Find out who did this. Bring me their names. Their faces. Their blood for his blood. Their names for his. Bring me something.*

DOYLE   We have all lost something, Paul. You came to me seeking justice. I open my file to you, and I say, "justice has been done." Do you see what I'm saying?

PAUL   Yes. I mean, I understand what you are "saying." You are saying you ordered my father's termination.

DOYLE   Not at all

PAUL   No, you are saying, "the men from AD killed" my father.

DOYLE   Well, I am saying your father—

PAUL   I don't believe you.

DOYLE   Well that is...

PAUL   I'll take these men.

DOYLE   "Take"?

PAUL   You say the men from AD. Say it again, not in here, not "between you and me," but in public, out there, where I need them, an inquiry, a Senate investigation, as a first step to restoring his—

DOYLE   That's—

PAUL   His name.

DOYLE   That's imposs—

PAUL   I want—

DOYLE   That's impossible.

PAUL   I want—names.

DOYLE "Names."

PAUL The names of the men who killed my father.

DOYLE I can't give—

PAUL Goddamn you, you can give me whatever it is I need. I need this.

DOYLE Paul, it isn't—

PAUL You *will* give me their names. He gave me the one thing, the only thing he knew I could use to protect him.

     PAUL hands DOYLE some papers.

DOYLE What is this?

PAUL This is Snowman, some of Snowman, photocopies of, of the codes, figures, I blacked out—but there is enough for you, or someone, to verify the, and I am willing, I will give you—in, exchange—

DOYLE "In exchange"—?

PAUL In exchange for *his* name, *their* names.

DOYLE For *this?*

PAUL My father believed in *this*, died for *this*. And I went to Ed Sparrow. I said I had Snowman and he told me to come to you, because you are the one who has to come forward, because you are an "honourable" man, and you will allow the truth to be told. He said you would help me.

DOYLE Ed Sparrow said this.

PAUL And, in exchange for your help, he would take Snowman.

DOYLE Ed Sparrow would.

PAUL   Yes. *Yes.* And he knows, and I will tell you, so that
                you know, that I will destroy Snowman if I am not
                given what I want.

DOYLE   And you think it's that simple.

PAUL   Yes, I do, think it's that simple, for you to send
                another cable. I do think that you can make
                something happen.

DOYLE   I'll have to…because this means nothing to me. Will
                you wait?

Scene Thirteen

---

*The listening room, an office adjacent DOYLE's:
DOYLE and SPARROW.*

DOYLE   Fuck you.

SPARROW   Mr. Doyle—

DOYLE   You said nothing of this.

SPARROW   I couldn't.

DOYLE   He comes to you, he says—

SPARROW   I couldn't acknowledge what he held, what he was offering.

DOYLE   So you send him—

SPARROW   We spoke through inference only.

DOYLE   Why didn't you *say?*

SPARROW   I had to know if he had Snowman.

DOYLE   In, in ex*change* for me?

SPARROW   I never said that.

DOYLE   He's bullshitting me, or what?

SPARROW   He may have inferred something which—

DOYLE   What the fuck did you say for him to infer?

SPARROW   I told you, he came to see me—

DOYLE   He gives you the same pitch, "I've seen so many people, no one will help me, help me."

SPARROW   That's right.

DOYLE   And you say what?

SPARROW   I suggest that someone at the CIA might be able to answer some—

DOYLE   Someone like me.

SPARROW   —some questions. He knew your name, Mr. Doyle.

DOYLE   And you tell him I will "answer some questions."

SPARROW   I say you will help him.

DOYLE   "Help" him.

SPARROW   That is all I—

DOYLE   And what did you *offer?*

SPARROW   Nothing.

DOYLE   I mean did you make a deal with this fuck or or—

SPARROW   There is no deal.

DOYLE   What did he *want?*

SPARROW   The same thing he asked from you, a Senate investigation.

DOYLE   And you what, you promised him, in exchange for my con-fucking-fession?

SPARROW Would you calm—can he hear any of this?

DOYLE *What?*

SPARROW Can he—

DOYLE No, are you fucked? Are you —? "Can he hear?" Jesus.

SPARROW Mr. Doyle, *please,* this *language.*

DOYLE Language? It's the way I fuckin'—Look. He comes to see you, and through "inference" says "I have the plans for Snowman," and you, through "inference," say "I want those plans," and—just a second—you, through *not* inference, send him to me for "help." You call me up, "I need to know does Paul Jackson have the plans."

SPARROW That's—

DOYLE "They could fall into the wrong hands."

SPARROW That's right.

DOYLE "He could go to the press."

SPARROW Yes.

DOYLE Alright: here is your answer. He *has* Snowman. Has he mentioned "wrong hands"? Has he mentioned "the press"? No. "I want a Senate investigation," he says, "names" he says, "names," *my* name—I mean what is this? What is it I am dealing with?

SPARROW You are jumping to conclu—

DOYLE I mean he thinks I am going to *testify* at a Senate *hearing* about how I had his father—like it's a given. Is it a given? Did you make a deal with—

SPARROW Calm down.

DOYLE Did you make a deal? Did you make—

SPARROW   No. I have told you. There is no deal.…I told Paul Jackson that you were an honourable man, and that you would act honourably.

DOYLE   You did.

SPARROW   I told him that the truth would be told, that you would testify, that you—that you would acknowledge that his father was your man in SI, that he turned, became a rogue agent.

DOYLE   All this you told him I would say.

SPARROW   I told him that you would explain how, with equal amounts of reluctance, regret and patriotism, you authorized Donald Jackson's termina—

DOYLE   No.

SPARROW   His termination.

DOYLE   *No.*

SPARROW   I told him you would do this.

DOYLE   What are you doing to me? What are you trying to do to me?

SPARROW   I am trying to make you accountable, Mr. Doyle, for your actions.

DOYLE   For *what?*

SPARROW   I think you have heard me. There are times, Mr. Doyle—John—when, for the good of the greater number, an individual must be sacrificed.

DOYLE   Sacrificed?

SPARROW   Donald Jackson understood that. He laid down his life to protect his own family.

DOYLE   I am not going to lie down.

SPARROW What are you now, John? What rank are you? GS12, isn't it?

DOYLE GS14.

SPARROW You testify, John, and you go to GS16, over*night*. You are a faceless cog, John, nothing, really, in the scheme. You picked up the phone this time; next time, someone else will pick it up. You sit there behind your desk and feel the power of your office. In fact, you have rather little power, John. The events which have unfolded these past few weeks would have occurred whether you had been involved in them or not. Events will continue to unfold. You will testify, Paul will give us Snowman, and the world will, once again—

DOYLE "Give us"?

SPARROW What?

DOYLE Paul will "give us"—you said, "give us" Snowman.

SPARROW That's right, he will give us the plans, to, in order to destroy them.

DOYLE To prevent them from falling into the wrong—

SPARROW That's right, from falling into—

DOYLE To keep him from going to the—

SPARROW Yes, the press.

DOYLE You fuck.

SPARROW John—

DOYLE Don't give me these bullshit excuses—"falling into the wrong"—there is no place on this earth Snowman can be made without us knowing about it. "Going to the press"—the press is filled everyday with stories of "the CIA killed my brother, my aunt, my dog," let him *go* to the press, let him *go* to "the wrong hands," this is bullshit, all of it.

SPARROW   You have to testify.

DOYLE   Tell me why. Tell me or, *right now,* I go back in there and it's *over.* Tell me why I testify, why, for what?

SPARROW   You must.

DOYLE   Why, it doesn't work, it doesn't work, you said to me, you grabbed the pencils and said—

SPARROW   Listen to me. This stays in this room. Do you under—what I am about to—

DOYLE   Whatever you say, it stays in the room.

DOYLE lets PAUL hear the following.

SPARROW   You have spoken of "jungles," of "watering holes." Of "survival." I am speaking of morality. I want you to know something. I was fourteen years old when we bombed Hiroshima. I took a vow the day I saw the pictures of Hiroshima, I swore that I would never allow this country to commit an act for which it could not be held accountable. There must be accountability. If we are to survive, as a people, there must be morality. Donald Jackson created a space defense system that would have made this country foolproof against Soviet attack. He didn't understand the implications of this. He didn't understand that he was giving us the ability to go nuclear without fear of retaliation. I couldn't let that happen. I supported his work because it offered this nation a vision of protection. I made sure that that vision would never achieve its actuality.

DOYLE   You faked tests.

SPARROW   If Snowman had ever been tested, succesfully, if we'd actually buried Snowman missiles in silos all over the continent, there'd've been nothing to prevent us from launching a first strike. If I had allowed Jackson to succeed, the Anti-Ballistic Missile Treaty would never have happened. Are you hearing this? I made it happen. I made the politicans resort to words, not guns, not missiles, but words, as a means to avoid our mutually-assured destruction. It was through failure we went forward. I accepted this as the only alternative to the unthinkable. These are difficult times, John, dangerous times. The people have seen the coming down of the wall, the end of the cold war, "the end of history," and therefore the end of us, of our utility, yours and mine and the institutions we represent. Yet we are faced with the prospect of a dozen little nations waking up after years of sleep to find beneath their feet weapons of mass destruction. With what will we protect ourselves? We have no treaties with these nations, or with the terrorists they are selling their weapons to. I *will* retire in two years, John. I *will* leave in place a system that is—that offers this nation protection.

DOYLE   You are telling me that Snowman can work?

SPARROW   I am telling you I need Snowman. To protect your jungle.

DOYLE   And I am going to testify so that you can have Snowman back?

SPARROW   You will survive, John. And, like your brother, you will be a hero. You see?

DOYLE   Oh yes…Sacrifices must be made.

Scene Fourteen

DOYLE's office, a moment later: DOYLE and PAUL.

DOYLE   You want to honour your father.

PAUL   Yes.

DOYLE   You want to honour what he was, truly was, which was a man of science—

PAUL   Yes.

DOYLE   —a man of peaceful intentions.

PAUL   That's—

DOYLE   This justice you seek, you believe it will, yes, restore to him his dignity.

PAUL   Yes.

DOYLE   I say it will not. I say it will further destroy a reputation you seek to rehabilitate. I say your father will be seen as the man who "got what he deserved." This will do nothing to further your mission. You tell me if I am incorrect. Okay. Paul: tell me what you want.

PAUL   I want...the names...

DOYLE   I want this: to hold your father up in death: to see to it that his vision is fulfilled, to take your gift, and put it in the hands of those who know what to do with such offerings, to announce to the world that your father provided us with the ability to make it snow in space, and right now, in this place, you and I hold the possibility of this in our hearts. And Paul, that is the key, that is the thing, "in our hearts," because—

PAUL   Yes.

DOYLE   The heart is the place we live, truly, and if we tell it lies, we will, sooner than later…

PAUL   The heart will explode.

DOYLE   We cannot tell ourselves lies, we have to admit what we want and take it. I want *you* to tell me, what you want.

PAUL   I want…

DOYLE   *Most*, what you want most: because you have *a* thing to give me, and I, in return, have *a* wish to grant you. And you should know this: the gift you will bring me: I do not want it for free.

PAUL   I don't want anything from—

DOYLE   No?

PAUL   I don't *want* anything.

DOYLE   Is there nothing?

PAUL   For my*self*? No.

DOYLE   You are "sure" of that.

PAUL   I'm here for my father.

DOYLE Yes, you came to me with the words, "I want to honour my father," you came to me with the thought, it may be, "I want justice for my father," but you came to me with the action, "I want something for my*self.*"

PAUL No.

DOYLE "I want to make amends for failing my father."

PAUL *No*, that isn't—

DOYLE Why did you keep the bag? Why, when according to your own words he begged you to destroy it, to *honour* him by burning the contents of that bag, why did you keep it? *Why,* when he said to you, "*burn this bag,*" why did you *keep* it? Because you knew, you understood that you sent that man to his death.

PAUL No…

DOYLE "Do something," you said, "protect me." And he did. Protected you. Your mother. Your daughter.

I know all about you, Paul. You are separated, one child, a reasonable mortgage; weekdays, a conducter of classes, speaker of lectures; poker every second Friday with your university friends; Saturday nights you get drunk and call your wife and ask her if you could come home now; on Sunday, you read *The New York Times*, your favourite section, "The Week in Review." You see pictures there of war and death and you wonder what you can do to stop it, but you realize, in your heart, you don't give a damn really, not enough to want to do something to stop it, not really enough at all, because you know you don't give a damn about the peasants and the poor, the refugees and the victims of torture, you have your life, it has been given to you and you like it, you are in love with your life and you want nothing to disturb the stillness of it, and if you are to have your life, the lectures and the poker and the sentimental drunkenness of it, you realize that there must be the poor and the peasants and the victims of torture, *fuck them.* You have your child and you love her very much, and the only reason your heart aches for the dying and dead children of war is that you see in their faces the face of your own daughter, you want to protect her, your own, not the others, and that is what your father taught us, protect your own, your *own*, not *them*; at this watering hole, fight to protect your own.

You'll give me the bag. I'll take the contents of the bag. There will be an inquiry into the activities of your father. It will be made clear that he was victimized, that, twenty-five years ago, his work on space defense was sabotaged, and that the saboteur was Ed Sparrow. Ed Sparrow faked tests. Ed Sparrow lied to Congress, and to this nation, his own people. It is Ed Sparrow who will be humiliated. It is Ed Sparrow who will be seen to have betrayed this nation. And, as his name sinks, your father's name will rise, *rise*, and, once we have built Snowman, it will soar into space. Paul…you will give me the bag.

PAUL   …I'll sit on a park bench, near a garbage can…

DOYLE   Paul…you did do. I mean, what I want to say to you is. You did what you were supposed to do.

PAUL   Yes.

DOYLE   You understand that?

PAUL   I. Yes. I want—to bring my father back. I want—to hold him. I want him to tell me, to help me, to teach me. I want… to thank you.

DOYLE   Well.

PAUL   But I can't. I know what you are, I know what you represent, a part of me as well and, I want to kill you, I want to see you suffer, I want to reach right over and kill you and a little piece of me as well.

DOYLE   I'm right here.

PAUL   No. I need you. I need that little piece of me.

DOYLE   This is how it begins. I see you in the distance, an unfamiliar form, fear seeps through my blood, you want what I have and I have three options: run from you, fight you, embrace you. But I want you to know, in this jungle, at this watering hole, there is plenty of water, you need only let me know who you are, open yourself up to me, I will embrace you, we will have peace, we will have an understanding, we need not thirst, not a single one of us. Stand up, Paul. Embrace me.

The End.